WILD WEATHER: OUR EXTREME PLANET
An Augmented Reality book

We've worked with experts and used the latest Augmented Reality technology to bring the awesome powers of nature to life—all in the palm of your hand. Set a tornado spinning, make a volcano erupt, or unleash an earthquake!

Augmented Reality is easy! Here's all you have to do …

1

Check that your computer has a **webcam** and that it can run the Augmented Reality (AR) software (see the minimum system requirements panel on the previous page).

2

Next, go online to the web site **www.parragon.com/bookscomealive** to download the AR software. Follow the on-screen instructions to install the software on your computer and then start the program!

3

As you go through the book, look out for special **AR panels,** which will tell you which trigger card to use. While the AR software is running, hold each trigger card in front of your webcam. Now watch as wild weather and the forces of nature come to life!

Need some help?

If you have a problem, check out our web site:
www.parragon.com/bookscomealive

FOUR AMAZING AUGMENTED REALITY EXPERIENCES!

Spin the EARTH to explore it, and play movie clips.

Send a TORNADO spinning on a trail of destruction!

Make the ground tremble with a mighty EARTHQUAKE.

See inside a fiery VOLCANO and make it erupt!

Picture credits

The publishers would like to thank the following sources for their kind permission to reproduce the pictures in this book.

Key: t=top, b=bottom, l=left, r=right, c=center

Alamy Images: 9br; Corbis: /Glowimages: 14–15, /Jeremy Horner: 25t, /Jim Reed Photography: 10–11, /NASA/Roger Ressmeyer: 6–7, /BPPT/Reuters: 25b, /Galen Rowell: 26–27, /Michael S. Yamashita: 22–23; Getty Images: 12, 15tr, 15r, 20, 20–21, 28–29, /AFP: 13t, 16b, 18, 19b, 21, 23c, 26b, /Ingólfur Bjargmundsson: 29, /Mitchell Funk: 23b, /NY Daily News: 14; iStockphoto: 7, 8, 8–9, 17, 19r, 27tr, 18–19, 30–31, 31; PA Photos: /AP, /AP Photo/Khalid Tanveer: 16-17; Photolibrary. com: 9c, /Warren Faidley: 12–13; Reuters Limited: /Ho New: 24–25; Rex Features: /Sipa Press: 27t; Science Photo Library: /Jim Reed Photography: 11c; US DoD: 13br

Movie clip credits
Tornado: Roger Hills/Science Photo Library
Volcano: iStockphoto.com
Earthquake: AFP/Getty Images

Text, design, and illustration
copyright © Carlton Books Limited 2012

This edition published by Parragon in 2013
Parragon
Chartist House
15–17 Trim Street
Bath BA1 1HA, U.K.
www.parragon.com

ISBN 978-1-4723-0768-2
Printed in Heshan, China

Executive editor: Paul Virr
Senior art editor: Jake da'Costa
Cover design: Jake da'Costa
Photoshop illustrators: Mark Walker & Jake da'Costa
Augmented Reality coordinator: Tracy Tsang
Creative director: Clare Baggaley
Picture research: Ben White
Production: Claire Halligan
Technical consultant: Dr. Frances Drake, School of Geography, University of Leeds, U.K.

WILD WEATHER WORDS

Experts use special words to describe wild weather and forces of nature. Any words that are highlighted in **bold** are explained in the glossary at the back of this book.

WILD WEATHER

OUR EXTREME PLANET

ANITA GANERI

PaRragon

Bath · New York · Singapore · Hong Kong · Cologne · Delhi
Melbourne · Amsterdam · Johannesburg · Shenzhen

RESTLESS WORLD

Our planet, the Earth, is a constantly moving and changing world. These changes can be violent and destructive, causing terrible disasters that make the news headlines. Some disasters are caused by extreme weather events, others are the result of natural forces deep inside the Earth.

This photograph of the Earth seen from space shows the swirling storm clouds of a hurricane over the Atlantic.

WIND AND WATER

Hot sunshine, wispy clouds, howling winds, pouring rain, and drifting snow all make up the weather we experience from day to day. Our weather happens in the lowest layer of the Earth's **atmosphere**, called the troposphere. The Sun's rays heat the surface of the Earth, which in turn heats the air in the troposphere. The heating is uneven, so the air gets warmer in some places than in others. These differences in temperature make the air move around, creating anything from a gentle breeze to a violent hurricane.

Water plays a big part in the weather. The clouds we see in the sky are made up of water, either small droplets of water or tiny ice crystals—billions of them. The water that forms clouds has evaporated from the seas and the land. This water falls on us as rain, hail, or snow. So water constantly moves into the atmosphere and then falls back to the ground. Weather experts call this the water cycle.

WILD WEATHER

Sometimes the movement of the air and the movement of water in the water cycle create extreme, wild weather events. These include **hurricanes**, **tornadoes**, heavy rainfall, **blizzards**, **heat waves**, **droughts**, and thunderstorms.

PLANET EARTH

Hold the world in your hands and discover where tornadoes, earthquakes, and volcanoes occur. Plus watch movie clips of these awesome events!

FORCES OF NATURE

The ground beneath us is a layer of solid rock called the Earth's **crust**. At its thickest, the crust is about 37 miles deep, so it is very thin compared to the size of the Earth. Below the crust is another layer of rock, called the mantle, which is thousands of miles thick. Some of the rock here is actually semimolten (semiliquid). Below the mantle is the Earth's core, which reaches temperatures of up to 9,932°F—that's more than 50 times hotter than boiling water!

The crust is not as solid as it seems. It is cracked into many giant pieces, called **tectonic plates**, which slide extremely slowly over the mantle below. Where the plates meet at their edges, molten rock from the mantle (called **magma**) often forces its way to the surface, forming **volcanoes** that eject **lava** and **ash**. Sudden movements of the plates cause **earthquakes**, and if these happen under the sea, they can set off giant waves called **tsunamis**.

Volcanic eruptions are some of the most dramatic signs of the powerful forces at work deep inside the Earth.

INSIDE THE EARTH

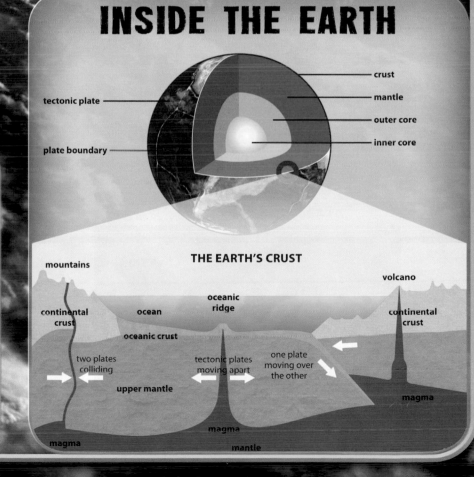

- crust
- mantle
- outer core
- inner core
- tectonic plate
- plate boundary

THE EARTH'S CRUST

mountains

oceanic ridge

volcano

continental crust

ocean

continental crust

oceanic crust

two plates colliding

tectonic plates moving apart

one plate moving over the other

upper mantle

magma

magma

magma

mantle

CLIMATE AND CHANGE

Climate is the pattern of weather in a particular place and how it varies over a long period of time. For example, a temperate climate brings warm summers and cool winters, with some rain throughout the year. A tropical climate brings hot and humid weather all year round, with heavy rain almost every day.

Over the last hundred years or so, the world has warmed very slightly and climates are beginning to change. This is known as **global warming** or **climate change**. The changes may be small, but their effects could be huge over the next decades. Some climate experts think that a temperature rise of only 4°F could cause sea levels to rise and major flooding. This could seriously affect food and water supplies around the world.

THUNDERSTORM

A bolt of lightning lights up the sky, followed by a deafening clap of thunder—a thunderstorm is breaking! Lightning is made by giant sparks of electricity jumping through the air. Thunder is the noise made as the air expands. It sounds scary but is not harmful. However, lightning can be deadly.

TOWERING CLOUDS

Thunderstorms begin when warm, moist air rises up through cold air higher in the atmosphere. The warm air is lighter than the cold air, so it floats upward. As the warm air cools, the water vapor in it turns to water droplets and ice crystals. When there is a lot of warm air, the air keeps rising, forming towering cumulonimbus clouds, which can be more than 6 miles high.

Cumulonimbus clouds build vertically as a thunderstorm develops over Hawaii.

DANGER, ELECTRICITY!

Strong air currents move up and down through the cloud. As they do, water droplets and ice crystals smash into each other. This creates an electrical charge on the droplets and crystals. Gradually, a positive charge grows in the top of the cloud, and a negative charge grows in the base of the cloud.

Finally, the electric charge jumps from the cloud in a flash of **lightning**. The flow of electricity heats the air to about 54,000°F— that's about five times hotter than the surface of the Sun. This makes the air rapidly expand, making the booming sound of **thunder**.

You can track how far away a thunderstorm is by counting the seconds between the flash of lightning and the clap of thunder. Every five seconds you count equals one mile.

Cloud-to-ground lightning strikes the city of Hong Kong, China, during a heavy thunderstorm.

CLOUD-TO-GROUND

The electric charge jumps between the base of a thundercloud and the ground below.

CLOUD-TO-CLOUD

Lightning jumps from the base to the top of a cloud, or from the base of one cloud to the top of another.

CLOUD-TO-AIR

Lightning jumps from a cloud to the air around it. This often happens alongside cloud-to-ground strikes.

LIGHTNING STRIKE

Although cloud-to-cloud lightning is the most common, cloud-to-ground lightning is the most dangerous, because it can strike trees, buildings, and people.

When lightning hits an object on the ground, a powerful electric current flows through the object, causing it to heat up. If lightning hits a tree, the electricity makes the tree's sap boil in an instant, blasting the tree apart. Lightning is responsible for starting many forest fires.

People hit by lightning are normally badly injured or killed, because they get a giant electric shock. This can cause severe burns and even a fatal heart attack.

A forest fire caused by a lightning strike in Yellowstone National Park, U.S.A.

GROUNDED

Lightning can also damage buildings. Many tall buildings have metal rods on their roofs, called lightning conductors. Because metal is such a good conductor of electricity, it channels the lightning safely to the ground, protecting the building.

Lightning strikes the lightning conductors on the Sears Tower and the John Hancock building in Chicago, Illinois, in 2008.

TORNADO

A tornado is one of the most extreme weather events on the planet. This violent, funnel-shaped storm spins across the ground, destroying everything in its path. With wind speeds of up to 310 mph, tornadoes smash houses to pieces, hurl cars high into the air, and leave a trail of debris behind them.

TWISTING WINDS

Tornadoes often occur where cold dry air meets moist tropical air. This can create massive rotating thunderstorms called supercells. Inside a supercell, strong winds blow in different directions at different heights. Sometimes this makes the air below the storm spin horizontally, level with the ground below.

Powerful rising and falling air currents can tip the spinning air up into the thundercloud, so that it spins vertically. When a strong downdraft pulls this spinning air downward and out of the base of the thundercloud, a rotating funnel-shaped cloud called a vortex appears. If the vortex reaches the ground, it becomes a tornado!

TORNADO

SET A TORNADO SPINNING BY PUTTING THE STEPS IN ORDER!

COLD DRY AIR

WARM MOIST AIR

STRONG WINDS

HORIZONTAL SPINNING AIR

RISING AND FALLING AIR

STRONG DOWNDRAFT

> "It made a thundering roar like a giant freight train."
> *Survivor of the Tri-State Tornado*

A tornado tears across the ground in western Kansas, part of the famous Tornado Alley.

The Tri-State Tornado that ripped through Missouri, Illinois, and Indiana on March 18, 1925, is the deadliest single tornado on record. It killed nearly 700 people and created a trail of destruction 215 miles long.

TORNADO ALLEY

Tornadoes can happen almost anywhere, but they happen a lot in Tornado Alley—a stretch of the United States running from Texas through Oklahoma, Kansas, Nebraska, and the Dakotas. About 700 tornadoes rip through this region each year. Many homes in the area have storm shelters that can withstand a tornado.

SEVERE WEATHER

SHELTER AREA

STORM CHASERS

Because tornadoes are such violent storms, they are difficult for scientists to study. To measure the forces at work inside tornadoes, scientists chase after them in fast vehicles equipped with special measuring equipment.

SEVERE W

RESEARCH

EXPLORER

TORNADO POWER

The strongest winds in the world are found in tornadoes. A tornado's strength, or intensity, is measured by the damage it does. Experts grade this intensity, using the Enhanced Fujita Scale. It was invented by Professor Theodore Fujita at the University of Chicago in 1971.

EF SCALE	WIND SPEED	DAMAGE
EF0	65–85 mph WEAK	
EF1	86–110 mph WEAK	
EF2	111–135 mph STRONG	
EF3	136–165 mph STRONG	
EF4	166–200 mph VIOLENT	
EF5	more than 200 mph VIOLENT	

HURRICANE

Hurricanes are massive, swirling storms that start over tropical oceans. The center of a hurricane, known as the eye, is relatively calm, but the weather surrounding it is wild, with thick clouds, heavy rain, and powerful, spiraling winds. Hurricanes are called cyclones in the Indian Ocean and typhoons in the Pacific.

A SPINNING STORM

A hurricane starts when a cluster of thunderstorms drifts over the warm ocean around the equator. The warm water heats the air above, causing it to rise very quickly. It then cools to form thunderclouds and rain. As the storm gets bigger, it starts spinning. If the wind speed of the tropical storm increases to around 74 mph, it becomes powerful enough to be classed as a hurricane.

A hurricane can measure almost 620 miles across with a circular **eye** up to 62 miles wide. If a hurricane reaches land, it can cause massive damage, but over land, it dies down in a few days. This is because it no longer has a supply of warm moist air to power it.

The eye in the center of Hurricane Wilma can be clearly seen in this satellite photograph of it spiraling toward the south of Mexico in 2005.

Hurricane Frances struck the coast of Florida in September 2005, causing serious flooding.

In October 1998, Hurricane Mitch struck Central America with winds blowing at more than 150 mph and heavy rains that caused catastrophic flooding and lethal **mudslides**.

HURRICANE FORCE

Hurricanes are measured according to how strongly the winds are blowing and how much damage they do when they hit land. Experts rate them using the Saffir-Simpson Hurricane Scale. A category 5 hurricane is the most powerful.

CATEGORY	WIND SPEED	STRUCTURAL DAMAGE
1	74–95 mph	Minor flooding along coasts. Little structural damage. Some damage to mobile homes and trees.
2	96–110 mph	Damage to roofs, windows, and doors. Some trees blown down. Small boats swept ashore.
3	111–129 mph	Damage to buildings. Mobile homes destroyed. Leaves torn from trees. Serious flooding.
4	130–156 mph	Roofs torn off and walls collapse. Beaches washed away. Large boats swept inland. Severe flooding.
5	157 mph or higher	Buildings destroyed by the wind, some near the coast swept away. Flooding up to 10 miles inland.

FROM A TO Z

The progress of hurricanes is closely watched, in order to warn people if they are approaching. To make hurricanes easier to identify and track, they are given names, such as Hurricane Emily. A new, alphabetical list of names is started every year. There are separate lists for each region. If a hurricane is particularly damaging, its name is never used again.

STORM HUNTERS

In the United States, "Hurricane Hunter" aircraft fly into hurricanes to collect data about their strength and direction. To reach the eye of a hurricane, the crew have to fly through the towering clouds around it, known as the eyewall. This is the toughest part of each mission, as the plane gets tossed around by thunderstorms and powerful winds.

BLIZZARD

Blizzards are deadly snowstorms that combine heavy snowfall with strong winds and biting cold. Snow is blasted along horizontally by powerful gusts of wind that can reach speeds of more than 35 mph. Blizzards can last for more than three hours, and they make traveling extremely hazardous.

SNOW HAZARDS

Blizzards occur when two air masses—one cold and dry and the other warm and moist—suddenly collide. The warm air is forced up over the cold air, creating violent snowstorms.

Blizzards can cause serious damage. Heavy snow can bring down power lines, bury cars and trucks, and smash roofs. Cities are brought to a standstill, and people are sometimes left without heat, water, food, and power. Because blizzards can blow up so suddenly, people may find themselves trapped in their homes, offices, or cars.

The extremely low temperatures that occur during blizzards also put people at risk of hypothermia (when body temperature drops below normal) and frostbite (when skin and body tissues freeze). People can die from both of these if they don't get treated quickly.

A blizzard brings heavy snowfall and strong winds to Yellowstone National Park, Wyoming.

In March 1993, a ferocious blizzard known as the "Storm of the Century" hit the United States. Over 3 feet of snow fell in some places, burying cars and making roads impassable.

WHITEOUT

The worst blizzards are whiteouts, where windblown snow makes it almost impossible to see. Because you cannot see the horizon or judge distances, it is easy to lose your bearings, so that you don't know where you are.

Iowa City, in February 2011. As the wind picks up, a blizzard becomes a whiteout and the horizon vanishes completely.

Europe has suffered unusually cold winters recently. Here, a snowplow clears the snow-covered streets of Berlin after a blizzard swept across Germany in January 2011.

CHILL FACTOR

One of worst dangers of blizzards is the windchill factor. This makes it feel colder than it actually is, and the stronger the wind, the colder it feels. For example, if the temperature is 39°F, and the wind speed is 30 mph, it can feel like 12°F.

WINDCHILL	DESCRIPTION
34°F to 14°F LOW	It feels slightly uncomfortable outdoors. Warm clothing, a hat, and gloves are recommended.
14°F to -13°F MODERATE	Feels cold on uncovered skin. Hat, gloves, and layers of dry, warm clothing are necessary. Being outdoors for long periods can be dangerous.
-13°F to -49°F COLD	All skin must be covered. Be active and move around to keep warm. Risk of hypothermia. Frostbite can occur very rapidly on uncovered skin.
-49°F to -75°F WARNING LEVEL	Dangerously cold. Outdoor activity should be limited to short periods. Severe risk of hypothermia. All skin should be covered up with suitable winter clothing since exposed skin freezes in minutes.
-76°F and colder VERY EXTREME	Conditions outdoors are extremely hazardous. High risk of hypothermia. Any exposed skin will freeze in just two minutes, so stay indoors.

BLIZZARD SURVIVAL TIPS

1. Stay indoors, out of the cold. If the power goes off, stay in one room for warmth.
2. If you're caught outside, take shelter or dig a snow cave. A snow cave can trap heat, just like the walls of an **igloo**.
3. Stay hydrated by drinking water, but don't eat snow, because it lowers your body temperature.
4. If you're caught in the car, don't get out and walk. Turn on the heater every few minutes, keeping a window open for fresh air. Tie something colorful to the car's aerial for rescuers to spot.
5. Wear layers of clothing. These will trap heat. Keep moving your arms and legs so that you stay warm.

FLOOD

Floods happen when water from rivers or the sea overflows areas that are usually dry land. Heavy rainfall can turn rivers into raging torrents, sweeping away everything in their path, while powerful storms can send giant waves of seawater inland—with catastrophic results.

WILD WATER

Floods are the worst result of wild weather. Each year they kill more people than any other natural disaster, including earthquakes and erupting volcanoes. Over the centuries, floods have claimed millions of lives.

A huge flood can be disastrous, sweeping away homes, roads, crops, and cars. **Stagnant** floodwater can also spread disease. Despite the risks, hundreds of millions of people around the world live on floodplains (the flat land alongside rivers that gets covered with water when it floods). The main reason is that the rich soil in these areas is good for growing crops.

In the summer of 2010, monsoon rains caused catastrophic flooding in Pakistan, destroying 1.7 million homes. This picture shows people being rescued by helicopter, surrounded by floodwater.

Survivors wade down a flooded road in central Pakistan during the August 2010 floods.

RIVER FLOODS

Melting snow or very heavy rain can cause a river to burst its banks and flood the surrounding land. The worst floods happen along the world's largest rivers, such as the Yangtze in China. In 1998, heavy **monsoon** rains caused floods that left 4,000 people dead and 15 million homeless.

FLASH FLOODS

Flash floods happen very quickly when heavy rain falls on a small area, such as in a valley or gorge. The rainwater gets funneled into a ferocious flow that can destroy everything in its path. Flash floods also happen in deserts, where dry riverbeds can suddenly turn into raging torrents.

COASTAL FLOODS

Coastal floods occur when tsunamis (earthquakes at sea) or violent storms raise the sea level so much that water sweeps inland. Most coastal floods are caused by tropical storms, such as hurricanes. These can cause a **storm surge**, raising the level of the sea by up to 16 feet.

FUTURE FLOODING

Climate change will make flooding more likely in some places. Sea levels are slowly rising, because of the melting polar ice caps and because the water in the sea expands as it warms. Higher sea levels make coastal flooding more likely during storms. Changes in climate could also mean heavier rains in some parts of the world, leading to more river floods and **flash floods**.

The flood barrier across the Thames river is a barrage that can be closed to protect London, U.K., from high tides and storm surges.

FLOOD DEFENSES

To protect against flooding, walls or embankments are sometimes built along riverbanks. These are called "levees" (from the French word for "raised") and are often built from soil and covered in grass, gravel, or concrete. Levees make the riverbank higher and stop water overflowing onto the floodplain.

Another type of flood protection is a barrage. This is a damlike structure, built across a river estuary. Its gates are usually left open to let river water flow out to sea, but they can be closed to stop storm surges moving back up the river to flood low-lying land.

SCORCHED EARTH

When a region suffers long spells of dry weather, a drought may happen. Without rain, the soil becomes dry and cracked, while plants wither and die. Even if some rain falls, there is not enough water to soak into the ground before it dries out again.

DEADLY DROUGHT

Droughts are a natural feature of the climate in many parts of the world, especially in places that normally have a low amount of rainfall. But they can be made worse by human activities, such as overfarming, cutting down large areas of trees, or the overuse of water.

Droughts can last for months or even, in extreme cases, for years, with terrible results. Water is vital for life, and water shortages can kill crops and animals. In poorer countries, droughts can lead to terrible famine, starvation, and disease. Dry soil breaks up and is easily whipped up by the wind into dust storms. There is also a greater risk of **wildfires**.

Women line up for food in a **refugee camp** in Somalia. Severe drought in East Africa in 2011 led to a devastating famine affecting Somalia, Ethiopia, and Kenya.

Drought has dried up the water of this lake in South Australia, killing the trees along its shoreline.

HEAT WAVES

A heat wave is a period of very hot weather that lasts much longer than usual. There may also be high humidity, so that it feels hot and sticky at the same time. Heat waves can be deadly. In Australia, they have killed more than 4,000 people over the last hundred years, making them deadlier than any other natural disaster.

High temperatures can cause serious health problems, such as heat exhaustion and life-threatening heatstroke, but it is not just the heat that makes people sick. When the wind drops in cities, dirt and fumes hang in the air. This creates a choking fog of polluted air, called smog, making it hard to breathe.

A cloud of smog hangs over Los Angeles, California. Smog can be a serious health hazard in large cities.

The 2003 heat wave led to drought and crop failures all across Europe.

HOTHOUSE EUROPE

In 2003, a heat wave hit Europe, bringing the hottest summer for 450 years. More than 40,000 people died—15,000 in France alone. Some parts of France had temperatures above 104°F for a whole week. In southern Portugal, temperatures hit 118°F, causing forest fires to break out. Three years later, another massive heat wave hit Europe. Britain had its hottest July ever, with temperatures reaching 98°F.

WILDFIRE

Giant, roaring wildfires can start from small beginnings. All it takes is a spark from a campfire during a hot summer's day, and moments later, fire can be raging through the dry grass and trees. Flames can spread through a forest faster than a person can run, destroying everything they encounter.

HOW FIRES START

Fires always start with a source of heat. In remote areas of forests, where there are few people, the most common cause of wildfires is lightning. The huge electric current that passes through a tree hit by lightning can set the tree on fire. In areas where people live or visit, most wildfires are started accidentally, either by campfires, discarded cigarettes, or sparks from machinery or fallen power lines. Some wildfires are even started deliberately.

FAST FLAMES

Once a wildfire has started, it spreads along a line of burning vegetation called a flame front. The flame front burns everything in front of it, leaving smoldering ashes behind. Winds and the slope of the ground control how fast the fire moves. With a wind behind it, a flame front can advance more than 6 feet each second. Flames spread more quickly uphill than downhill.

The fiercest wildfires spring up where there is thick, superdry vegetation. The burning is so intense that it sends hot air swirling high into the atmosphere, creating strong winds and even mini-tornadoes, called fire devils, or fire tornadoes.

A flame front advances through the dry vegetation north of Los Angeles in the Station Fire of 2009.

WILDFIRE ZONES

Wildfires are most common in places that experience hot, dry summers, and where there is forest, scrubland, or grassland. The world's wildfire hot spots are the west of North America and the southeast of Australia. In these areas, the summer is known as the "fire season." The hot weather dries out the vegetation, and warm, strong winds blow regularly. As the climate warms, many scientists expect that wildfires will become more common.

BLACK SATURDAY

In February 2009, the Australian state of Victoria was bone-dry. No rain had fallen for months on end, and a record-breaking heat wave made conditions perfect for wildfires to start. On February 7, strong winds toppled electricity power lines, starting many small fires. In the wind, they quickly grew into a massive wildfire that tore through the bush, engulfing several towns. In all, 173 people were trapped and killed by smoke and flames. The day became known as "Black Saturday."

Firefighters monitor the progress of the 2009 Station Fire as it approaches the city of Los Angeles, California.

FIGHTING FIRE

Firefighters use different ways to stop a fire spreading, including clearing gaps in the forest that fire cannot cross, called firebreaks. These are made with bulldozers and hand tools. Firefighters can also drop chemicals called fire retardants from aircraft onto trees to slow down the spread of a fire. On the ground, firefighters use water hoses and beaters to try to put out flames.

A plane drops red fire retardant onto the trees to slow the progress of a wildfire in the south of France in 2006.

EARTHQUAKE

Earthquakes are among nature's most destructive forces, capable of flattening cities and killing or injuring thousands of people. Suddenly, the earth trembles and cracks, or lurches up and down, sending buildings crashing to the ground and burying streets, cars, and people under rubble.

The 1995 earthquake in Kobe, Japan, caused the collapse of more than 200,000 buildings across the city.

SHOCK WAVES

Earthquakes happen when the tectonic plates of the Earth's crust jostle each other, putting the rocks under strain. Sometimes, the plates lock together, causing the forces to build up. Then they suddenly give way, releasing the pressure as an earthquake. Most earthquakes happen at plate boundaries, where deep cracks, known as **faults**, form in the Earth's crust.

The point deep underground where the rocks slip is called the hypocenter. From here, shock waves of energy spread out through the ground. Directly above the hypocenter is the epicenter. This is the point on the surface where the earthquake's effects can be felt and seen.

EARTHQUAKE

The earth-shattering force of an earthquake is in your hands! See the destruction caused by different strengths of earthquake.

NORMAL FAULT

Two plates pull apart. One plate slides under the other.

REVERSE FAULT

Two plates push together. One slides up over the other.

STRIKE-SLIP FAULT

Two plates slide past each other, in opposite directions.

Experts test an earthquake early-warning system, checking a seismograph screen for signs of shock waves.

MEASURING QUAKES

Tens of thousands of earthquake tremors shake the Earth each year, but thankfully, most are too small to be felt. About a hundred are strong enough to cause some damage, while around ten are seriously earth-shattering. Earthquake experts called seismologists use the Moment Magnitude Scale (MMS) to grade earthquakes. It measures the energy that is released by an earthquake on a scale from one to ten.

QUAKE PROOF

A major cause of death during earthquakes is collapsing buildings, so architects have been designing buildings that are better able to stand the shaking. One of the most famous quake-proofed buildings is the Transamerica Pyramid in San Francisco, California. Its shape makes it very stable, plus it sits on underground rollers that let it rock gently.

The Transamerica Pyramid swayed during an earthquake in 1989, but it did not fall down.

TSUNAMI

An earthquake under the sea can trigger a tsunami—a series of giant waves that race across the sea. At first, the waves are low, but as they near land, they slow down and build up to a great height. Then massive walls of water crash down onto the shore, washing people, buildings, and vehicles away.

HOW A TSUNAMI HAPPENS

Tsunamis are usually caused by earthquakes under the sea. These cause a sudden shift in the seabed, forcing a huge volume of water upward. Tsunamis can also be triggered by undersea volcanoes or landslides, creating giant waves.

series of low waves

waves build in height

①

②

sea level

shallows

shock waves

① The shock sets in motion a series of waves that race across the ocean at speeds of up to 590 mph—as fast as a jet plane. At this stage, the waves are usually less than 3 feet high and may be hundreds of miles apart.

② As the waves reach the shallow water by the shore, they slow down. The tops of the waves move faster than the bottoms, making the waves rise up to great heights before crashing down onto the shore.

A tsunami wave crashes over a street in Miyako City, Japan, after a massive earthquake struck in March 2011.

DEADLY WAVES

A huge wall of water isn't always the first sign of an approaching tsunami. If the trough (low point) between the wave crests reaches the coast first, it pulls the water away from the shore, exposing the seafloor. This is an important warning sign—the waves may be less than five minutes away.

The danger does not pass with the first wave that hits land. It may be followed by many others, between 10 and 45 minutes apart. These follow-up waves can push the water almost a mile inland.

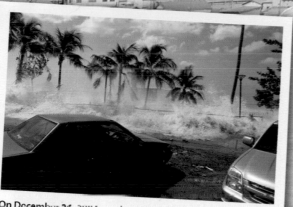

On December 26, 2004, a colossal 9.3 magnitude earthquake off the coast of Indonesia triggered a massive tsunami. Around 300,000 people died.

TSUNAMI WARNING

Most tsunamis happen in the Pacific Ocean. They are tracked by the Pacific Tsunami Warning Center in Hawaii. A series of pressure sensors on the seabed measure the weight of water above them. If a tsunami passes, the sensors send signals to a chain of buoys sitting on the surface. These beam the information to a satellite, which signals the alarm to an early-warning center.

AVALANCHE

With a gigantic roar, a huge slab of snow breaks loose and hurtles down a mountainside at high speed. Nothing can stop an avalanche in full flow. As it travels downhill, it gets even faster, burying everything in its path under thick snow: cars, buildings, and whole villages. Escape is almost impossible.

SNOW MOTION

Avalanches occur when a mass of snow suddenly breaks loose and crashes down a mountainside. They are most common after a large fall of fresh, powdery snow. The snow piles up quickly, overloading the icy slab underneath and causing it to crack. This makes the soft snow above unstable, and it starts to slip and slide. Many avalanches are triggered by the movements of walkers or skiers, but lots of other things can set them off, including a gust of wind or a noise, such as a car door slamming.

RACE AGAINST TIME

Avalanches can race downhill at more than 186 mph, making them almost impossible to outrun. The chances of being rescued alive from an avalanche are low. The snow sets like concrete, making it impossible to move. Most people survive if they are dug out in 15 minutes. But after 45 minutes, only a quarter survive. Search and rescue teams have to work fast to find survivors and dig them out.

Rescue teams use long sticks called snow probes and specially trained dogs with sensitive noses to find survivors buried under the snow.

On February 23, 1999, a huge avalanche crashed down on the village of Galtür in the Austrian Alps, burying buildings and killing 31 people.

SNOW-PROOF

In avalanche danger zones, various ways of reducing the risk have been tried. These include setting off explosives to deliberately trigger small, controlled avalanches, which prevents larger buildups of snow.

Steel fences, nets, dams, and bridges are often built in avalanche-prone areas, and rows of trees are planted across mountain slopes to hold back any falling snow.

AVALANCHE SURVIVAL

* If you are going into an avalanche risk area, wear a rescue beacon that signals where you are.

* If you're caught in a snowslide, try to grab onto a rock or a tree.

* If you're being swept away, try to "swim" to the surface.

* Close your mouth so that you don't swallow too much snow.

* If you're buried, keep one hand in front of your face to keep an air space free.

FUTURE FALLS

Although global warming may mean less snow, it could mean more avalanches. Higher temperatures in mountains could lead to more freeze–thaw cycles of snow. This creates an icy, slippery top layer, so that new snowfall can slide easily downhill in an avalanche.

huge avalanche crashes violently own the side of the mountain K2 in e Karakoram Range, Pakistan.

VOLCANO

An erupting volcano is a spectacular sight. Glowing rivers of molten rock, called lava, burst from beneath the Earth's crust, sometimes with terrifying explosive force. Towering clouds of, ash and thick landslides of mud, add to its devastating impact.

LETHAL LAVA

A volcano occurs at an opening in a weak spot of the Earth's crust, where molten rock, called magma, bursts or leaks out. When magma reaches the surface, it is called lava. Different types of lava cause different types of eruption and form different shapes of volcano.

There are roughly 50 volcanic eruptions around the world each year, but the Earth has around 1,500 active volcanoes in total. About half of these can be found in an area around the Pacific Ocean called the "Ring of Fire." Volcanoes on land make up only about a third of all volcanoes; the rest occur under the sea.

VOLCANO

Take a look inside a mighty stratovolcano. Then make it blow its top in a violent and fiery eruption!

The Soufrière stratovolcano on the Caribbean island of Montserrat violently erupted in 1997.

STRATOVOLCANO

crater

alternate layers
of lava and ash

9,843 feet

SHAPE: Tall and symmetrical cone shape with steep sides.
MADE FROM: Alternate layers of thick lava and ash that have built up over centuries of eruptions.

CINDER CONE

layers of
volcanic
fragments

1,640
feet

SHAPE: Small, rounded cone shape with very steep sides.
MADE FROM: Cinders ejected in mild eruptions. Often found on the sides of other volcanoes.

SHIELD VOLCANO

old lava flows

new lava flows

16,400 feet

central vent

SHAPE: Wide and low dome shape, with gently sloping sides.
MADE FROM: Thin, runny lava that flows for tens of miles before cooling and setting hard.

VOLCANIC HAZARDS

Lava flows: Lava can reach temperatures of 2,192°F and usually destroys everything in its path. However, it rarely kills people, because it does not flow very fast.

Pyroclasts: These are rocks hurled out from volcanoes. The biggest are volcanic "bombs" that can be fist-sized or bigger.

Ash clouds: An eruption can blast out awesome quantities of ash. The ash travels on the wind, burying towns, fields, and people when it falls.

Pyroclastic flows: These are lethal avalanches of ash and gas that flow down the sides of volcanoes at great speed. Anything caught up in them is destroyed.

Lahars: These are massive mudflows formed when volcanic ash mixes with water. They can sweep downhill for hundreds of miles before setting hard like concrete.

ASH CLOUD CHAOS

Eyjafjallajökull (say: Ay-uh-fyat-luh-yo-kuut-lul) is a stratovolcano in Iceland. In March 2010, a series of small earthquakes warned that an eruption was likely. The volcano then erupted twice, creating a cloud of volcanic ash over 5 miles high. As the ash cloud spread over northern Europe, it caused chaos, grounding flights and leaving passengers stranded.

CLIMATE CHANGE

The Earth's atmosphere is slowly getting warmer. This change is called global warming. As the temperature rises, the world's climates are being affected. Many scientists believe that climate change is caused by human activities.

THE EVIDENCE

Weather records collected carefully for hundreds of years show us that the Earth's atmosphere is warming. Over the last hundred years, its average temperature has increased by 1.45°F. This doesn't sound like a lot, but an increase of just a few degrees could have a devastating impact on our planet and its climate.

We can see some effects of climate change already. For example, the world's glaciers are slowly melting, and the ice covering the Arctic Ocean is shrinking every year. Sea levels are rising, too—in the last century, they have risen between 4 and 10 inches. Patterns of rainfall are changing, with more rain falling in some places and less in others.

Climate change and the melting of the polar ice caps could affect the survival of many creatures, such as polar bears.

THE EFFECTS

Some people blame climate change for natural disasters, such as hurricanes and floods, but we can't be certain if it is the cause of individual weather events. However, climate change is likely to cause major problems in the future, especially if we do nothing to stop it.

Climate change could make floods, blizzards, and droughts more common. Changes in temperature and rainfall could affect crops, causing drought and famine in the drier areas of the world. A rise in sea level could have the greatest impact, affecting millions of people. Low-lying coastal areas, such as Bangladesh, would be flooded more regularly, and many coastal cities would become uninhabitable.